EMBRACE THE SPECTACLE

A COMPASSIONATE INVESTIGATION OF TRAUMA & RECOVERY

ABERDEEN VIOLET &
SEVEN VIOLET

Published by The Mental Foundation
Cover art by Aberdeen Violet

www.wetwistedtrees.com
www.thementalfoundation.org

This book was composed
during the Coronavirus Pandemic of 2020.

Thank you
to my husband, Elliott,
& to our daughter, Ivy.
I could not have prescribed myself
more brilliant characters for life-sharing.
I love you both infinitely. I love our little spectacle.

Contents

DISSOCIATED ASSOCIATES

I'm Aberdeen. Seven wrote the first section of this book & I the second. There are several of us in here—in this brain, sharing this body. This particular classification of human is psychologically referred to as having 'Dissociative Identity Disorder' (formerly 'Multiple Personality Disorder'), or 'DID.' It is formed from repeated abuse in development. When the psyche was too tortured & strained from fear & violence, the brain fragmented, & 'alters' were formed. We grew as one being, divided into isolated pieces, separated by amnesia. We lived for years unaware of each other's existence (& therefore, memories & experiences, perspectives, fears, interests, pain). When any of us found ourselves 'in the front' (experiencing life & in control of the body's behavior), unable to trace, recall, or corroborate what had transpired when another alter had been in front, each assumed we had somehow forgotten. The true forgetting was in the original splitting—the compartmentalized collections of pain memories intentionally hidden. In order to remember the universal truth & birthright of belonging, 'I' had to remember the collective truth (through each alter's investigation) of my heart's past pain, & release it. I saw that I could either continue to exhibit my personalized manifestations of inherited unconsciousness, or choose to transform the energy through living in openness, honesty, & acceptance. I had been trying to peer into the abyss of my belief systems for years, while mired in confusion & self-sabotage. Without trust, it is incredibly difficult to transition from suffering to freedom. Feeling raw pain so that it can release itself from our psyches & bodies is understandably something we have conditioned ourselves to cover & run from. We are afraid of the feelings. The ominous pain presents as though it will never end if we enter its realm. We ignore our pain exactly as we began to when it was too hard for us to look. We believe we are protecting ourselves (& others) by keeping it hidden…but it is not hidden. It appears in our reactions—in violent behavior & thought. Trapped pain is not a compliant prisoner, & will govern its captor's life until set free. We think our way into a complex labyrinth of beliefs, cunningly designing itself to prevent us from finding our way out.

Our thoughts charm us, soothe us, scare us, convince us, bind us. When we are 'alone with our thoughts,' we believe we are hidden in solitude, yet there are so many of us hiding in solitude—intoxicated, manipulated, & misled by our thoughts. We 'know,' we 'figure it out,' we time travel, we strategize, we worry, we justify, we blame, we describe, we exit our lives.

This is what is happening now. Your present experience is thrilling or bland, provocative or disarming, sullen or joyous…It doesn't matter! It came from something else, became this, & will transform again. Trusting this impermanence helped me wring self-imposed significance out of every circumstance—from tragic hellacious abuse or euphoric pleasure to trivial passing things. We choose to let ourselves be tricked & swept away by our thoughts, memory, & imagination. We choose to accept or resist our emotions. The awareness witnessing our choosing is the center, source, god, nature, oneness, sameness, belonging, truth, light. It is the serene permanence of love's acceptance. It is available beneath, within, & throughout everything. All else is temporary—flowing, changing, transforming. We come in where we come in as we come in. We grow, develop, see, experience, interpret, & describe. If our survival is continuously threatened in development, the brain silences the heart so that its strategies for survival are clearly heard & commands followed. If we simply accept what is as it is (for which the compassionate heart is needed far more than analytical thought), our intuition will make all decisions necessary to flow in alignment with nature & all her dancing systems. Accepting everything about ourselves & each other includes our deepest human pain & seemingly unfathomable behavior. The confusion comes not from deeds done, not from skewed manifestations of insecurities & fear; but from our interpretations of them, & what we decide to make them mean about ourselves. This perspective does not excuse ugly human behavior; it allows for all manner of human manifestation, & grants us all endless opportunity to choose compassion, thereby influencing others with compassion.

My daughter has granted me an undeniable opportunity to dissolve & transform the deep darkness of generational trauma. I am honored she came through me, & delighted to nurture her. I do not possess or control her. She is nature's child, as we all are, & she is pure magic! May she always wander curiously! She will not be preyed upon & bound by her mother's unconsciousness. She is accepted here exactly as she is. If/when she seems to have forgotten, she will be reminded of her belonging. She will be reminded she is infinite, participating in the infinite.

We cannot be divided, yet we separate ourselves from ourselves & each other to survive our pain, which creates immense suffering. Humanity folds in on itself when it places its collective attention on division, separation, comparison, & judgment, instead of on acceptance & love. We are made of love. Love cannot be divided.

I perceive that all alters in my being are of the same psyche, body, heart, & mind. We know (now, after years of therapeutic endeavors & resistant self-destruction) that when we 'switch,' whomever presents in front is accepted & whatever happens is simply what happens. We have recently learned to see & acknowledge each other's pain & memories as 'the body's' experience, & therefore 'mine.' I didn't know about the violent violations which had transpired while other alters were in front, just as they were entirely unaware of my experiences with fear & violence. When we can feel & see the whole in context, we can cultivate compassion for our collective experience through acceptance. We embody it together. We are no longer fragments of a child defensively living to survive my mother, & I am no longer defensively living to survive myself/selves. It is possible to remove oneself from the clutches of past trauma once we realize we constructed the talons & operate their merciless manner ourselves.

Can we witness & accept each other's pain in our species? Everything any human has ever done is within your & my potential. We cannot integrate within humanity & recognize oneness if we remain loyal to conditioned wiring within us which encourages separateness & fearful defensive thinking. We have learned to dissociate from ourselves & from each other.

This is neither a book about Dissociative Identity Disorder, nor the specific damage done to elicit its complex creation. It is a book of healing. It encourages acute awareness, & freedom from suffering. There is no blame, shaming, or judgment. Salvation comes with acceptance & love. Abundant vitality, mercy, & light heal us when we repeatedly focus our attention on our hearts. Feel. Listen. Hearts are powerful, resilient drummers…

EMBRACE
THE SPECTACLE

Part I (by Seven Violet)

PLEASE REMEMBER

Remember.
(...for all women:)

You are brilliant, brave, loving, & wise. A brilliant, brave, loving, wise woman has the capacity to stand in her power, to approach & be approached with love in all her relations. This loving approach allows her to discern where she ought & ought not spend her life energy. A brilliant, brave, loving, wise woman must not forget that she is brilliant, brave, loving, & wise. When she forgets, fellow forgotten souls wander in as their shadows, to dance with her in the forgotten place. She must feel & she must remember. She must honor her light, her courage, her heart, & her power. She is brilliant, she is brave, she is loving, & she is wise.

AN ACT OF LOVE

As a little girl, I believed voicing my truth would betray my perpetrator. She terrified me. As a girl turned woman, I believed voicing my truth would betray my perpetrator, & what I carried of her inside me terrified me. My perpetrator behaved as forgotten, so she raised me as a shadow. I lived in a forgotten place. The earth's nature encouraged me to listen to & remember what I had learned to silence & forget.

My mother's violations of my body/mind/heart/ psyche composed the original betrayal in my experience of humanity, this lifetime. Hers was not a heart, but a heart's shadow. Although I tangled with many shadows thereafter, the only one who rivaled treating me worse than hers was my own. Continued self-abandonment has been a far greater betrayal. In order to heal, I traced self-betrayal all the way back to my choosing it in order to survive. I did not wish to live with her in lies, in our isolated violence—separate from the rest of the family in the very same house, separate from the world. I longed to be an authentic autonomous entity, pulsing with curiosity, open to opportunity, living in light. My wish was not an opportunity then; I was in shadow training. I chose to adhere. *I grew as a shadow in order to survive.*

The violence which continued in the privacy of this relationship was criminal & staggeringly heartbreaking. Truth is the most inspiring light of all—not informational truth; intuitive truth. It guides us to love. It has been evasive & mysterious, & nevertheless fueling my resilient engine. I want truth for everyone—authentic connection, heart-guided behavior, life without fear. Choosing to expose my truth, & share my shift from secretive entrapment & self-destruction to exalted freedom & love is not a betrayal of my mother as I had feared & imagined; it is an act of love—self-love, love for her, love for all women, & love for humanity.

My wish is that as people begin to speak & behave more authentically, we will find ourselves in each other & each other in ourselves. We will transfer priority from how something appears to be, & the interpreted meanings it collects, to how something simply is. We will move from frightened ego to opened heart. We will forgive. We will release resentments. We will not be afraid of what we perceive as our ugliness, our monstrous feelings, & the painful events of our collective & individual pasts. We will not abandon ourselves. We will no longer feel responsible for protecting our painful secrets. We will no longer feel compelled to impose control over others. Our behaviors, which grow from love or fear, ultimately feed love or feed fear. We each inform the collective with our words & behaviors. We, all parts of this magical unified system, have conned ourselves into believing we are separate.

FORGETTING

Trauma sends us into our minds, away from our hearts.

A traumatic event has occurred not when something painful has happened, but when the painful something has not been properly metabolized—the nervous system (& in humans, the thinking mind) has not been returned to a sense of homeostasis. Wild animals who are preyed upon, for example, exorcize their fears from being chased by lying down when they reach a safe space & 'running' with their muscles to rid their bodies of excess adrenalin. They are free immediately thereafter to resume typical activities. Humans, through our beautifully complicated ability to conceptualize, analyze, deconstruct, imagine, & attribute meaning to story, often attempt to process traumatic events through thinking. When left to our own devices, we store the frightened hormonal energy in our bodies—holding ourselves hostage in a purgatory realm of fight or flight, setting ourselves up for disease & psychosomatic reactivity. We cover painful feelings with an avalanche of thought. Hyper-vigilance (through familiarity) becomes our homeostasis. The entire system becomes further & further recalibrated. Perhaps more disturbingly, we *decide* (especially from trauma in early development) that each traumatic event uncovers or further confirms something fundamentally negatively true about ourselves or the world, with which we will henceforth agree—a false belief. False beliefs might tell us: we're not worthy of love, attention, or kindness; people are cruel & not to be trusted; we must not speak or demonstrate emotion; we are never safe. As we grow, our perspectives, thoughts, & behaviors develop in accordance with these false beliefs, keeping us separate & disconnected from other people & from our own curiosities. We have kept ourselves hidden, so we feel as though we don't belong. When we feel as though we don't belong, we hide.

In development, we learn from the words, energies, & behaviors of those around us. The feelings we have in response are internalized, interpreted through our limited vocabularies, & displayed through our limited emotional capacities.

A river forms as water finds the least difficult path to travel. That river broadens in dimension & force, as its movement continues & the earth accommodates to allow its continued passage. In the same manner, our impulsive thoughts & behaviors develop in our early years, & broaden in dimension as our analytical capabilities become more sophisticated (faster & complex, not wise or more conscious). We are conditioned. Traveling these rivers becomes conclusive, reliably guiding us to what becomes our cultivated emotional climate, our sea. Our sea is filled (over time) with the consequences carried by our rivers, & is maintained by our unconscious adherence to their force & power. It can feel as though we are subjugated by them. We forget that we established their shape & direction, we encouraged their speed, & we used them for survival. A stormy emotional climate is an inevitable result of surviving repeated trauma. We live in the weather of the climate we've created inside.

Each time a child is violated, terrorized, or otherwise devastated (shamed, criticized, neglected), the child's mind creates a story of explanation, protecting the heart & body from experiencing (& effectively processing) intense feelings. Years later, the adult version of that same child has likely kept her relational world isolated & inauthentic—walled off from love & intimacy so that she can adequately shield herself from pain. Her trust is mangled, intuition bastardized, & vulnerability guarded. Vulnerability is the universal language of the heart. In order for the heart to be susceptible to love, it must also be susceptible to attack. In cases of abuse throughout development, we learned to anticipate attack consistently & conceptualized love conditionally. We did not experience love unconditionally. We became fearful, skeptical, & calculating. The unfolding of subsequent life experiences need not follow suit. We ought not live in alignment with data gathered from experience to arrange predictions; in doing so (although we believe we are protecting ourselves), we resist spontaneity, which is how life freely happens. We experience interactions in relating to others through a suspicious, darkened perspective. Our minds guard our hearts & we live in thought instead of feeling—analysis & story instead of love. Loving energy is not ever gone. It is always available, but will seem elusive if we are wired to seek familiar discomfort in isolation instead, concluding that's all there is.

Our natural state is openness & presence, where love flows & joy is always possible. Fortunately, we survived. Unfortunately, we don't clearly recognize until much distress & wreckage has transpired in adulthood that the tools we used to survive are defense-based, & have thereby been preventing us from openness & presence.

VIOLENCE

Separateness invites comparison. Comparative thoughts are a form of violence.

Separateness makes us ill. We long for connection. We long to be seen, heard, & accepted. We long to give & receive love. False beliefs work to keep us alone & isolated, further confirming our non-belonging. Alone, as individuals, we become more fearful & defensive, & more convinced we ought to be alone. Isolation, loneliness, & a desire for acceptance & belonging, can manifest dangerously in societies through organizations supporting false belief systems—fear-based groups which discriminate against a specific race, religion, sexual orientation, or gender identity, for example. Whether placing oneself below or above others, there is a bold arrogance in believing one is separate, different, or special. Although we each possess unique characteristics through our genetics & our choices, humanity includes all people. Whether one feels a kick of inferiority or superiority, in isolation or in a righteous group of some ego-driven persuasion, one is still removing oneself from true community & authentic communication within the species one is, in fact, one of.

Deciding we are better or worse, above or beneath, is based on a network of comparisons & judgments, forming a stealth system of violence. Superiority & inferiority provoke distain toward others, masking an inner violence toward the self (shame, insecurity). Atrocities such as war, genocide, rape, & hate crimes are obvious pronounced examples of violence. They are the outwardly manifested results of violent judgmental thought, grown stronger in force over time.

We all have the capacity for violence. We use our separateness to justify further, in arrogance, our difference—our non-belonging. However, if we didn't belong here, we wouldn't be here, because what is *is*. Everything on this planet is of Earth. The Universe is made up of all it contains. If we learn in development that we are separate (through the inner violence of superiority, inferiority, or both), how can we know belonging? We hide how we feel from others, & posture to convince others our lives contain what they do not (social media is a fantastic breeding ground for this, but the practice of such posturing is certainly not new). We inauthentically relate in order to feel like we belong, but the feeling of not belonging continues. *We belong exactly as we are.* It's not surprising, then, that trying to fit what we aren't into the hole shaped for what we are fails us. To belong here, our initial inherent truth, our birthright, seems to have been taken from us by proxy. It was not taken! With learned wrath we pitted against ourselves, we decided we must not have deserved belonging, & we gave belonging up.

DECISIONS

We decided.

We chose all of this—individually & altogether. We have always chosen (& we continue choosing) how we behave & how we respond to circumstance. Each decision we make springs forth from either conscious presence, or unconsciousness informed by our violent conditioning & false beliefs. So, although in retrospect some choices seem to have not been conscious choices, they were our choices nonetheless, & are therefore our responsibility. When we are connected to trust, the universe, faith, god, higher power, source, oneness—whatever you might prefer to call the unification of it all, our intuition guides us in clear presence. We don't have trouble with decision-making, as the question of what to do or what not to do does not present itself; we are compelled or not compelled; we do or don't do. When we live in presence, we don't get dragged around by our belief systems. We don't make decisions to sabotage our lives, keeping ourselves small, isolated, frightened, & 'safe.' By continuously choosing presence instead of abandoning ourselves, we effectively abandon belief systems which have been programming our navigation. We can then feel & acknowledge the divinity of belonging.

We chose all of it, & we continue choosing. This is neither blame, nor harsh heartlessness; this is opportunity through valiant compassion. Nothing in your head is happening to you; you are choosing to listen & agree. You are choosing to ride the train, spin the record, watch the movie. Choose presence. Choose to investigate. Choose wonder, curiosity, inspiration, inquiry. Choose openness, vulnerability, expansion. Choose possibility. Choose to find what you want & move toward it. Choose grace. Choose mercy & forgiveness. Choose love.

Choosing love over fear is our responsibility.

Good vs Evil is a prevalent theme in all aspects of our conditioning—religion; books, films, & fairy tales; politics & war; intergroup & interpersonal relationships. As we are all of an original source, we are born neither Good nor Evil. We are Love. From there, we are conditioned. We remain open, or we close to protect ourselves. So the theme is more accurately: Love vs Fear. 'Evil' people's behaviors are inspired by fear. They are afraid. They became fearful because they are made of love & experienced pain—at the hands of someone else made of love who experienced pain & was behaving fearfully.

The true poison of a traumatic event is that we make it mean something so fundamentally negatively 'true,' that our entire perspective darkens & closes in. We are all responsible for our own behavior. Someone else's behavior has nothing to do with you, even if it is directed at you. A violation done to you is not about you. You are not responsible for that fearful person's or group's behavior. You are responsible for the fear it creates in you as a result of the meaning you have given the circumstance. You are responsible for whatever behavior you engage in as a result of your own accumulated fear.

SECRETS

Dear Ancestors:
I feel what lived in you. It is clear that an energetic map of our collective past led us here, hiding these cycles—suppressing with further lies, dressed up in different reasons, but increasingly & undeniably brutal. We can't go any faster or slower than we do. We accept, or we resist. Resistance builds strong

armies with the shadows of frightened children.
Acceptance gives love & light to fearful successions.
With acceptance, we introduce new conscious experi-
ences & behaviors into the vortex which will begin to
challenge the dark power of its swirling magnitude.
Courage is required to love our fears. Nurturing our
fears back to love is required for change. Thank you
for all lessons.

It is frightening to address our traumas & fears, as revelation defies the imposed secrecy of the system. We each made a silent, self-sacrificing promise to serve a corrupt arrangement. We were sworn in. Toxic energy is contained, protected, & encouraged in the dark environment of secrecy. If we share our truths as we heal, we can most authentically show others how to heal from similar wounds. Breaking systems of fear & secrets further opens possibility for change throughout humanity. Contrary to commiserating, we do not remain in the energy of the unconscious events; we look into them with compassion in order to transcend how their energy has impacted our belief systems. When belief systems are uprooted, perspectives shift. Compassion invites acceptance & forgiveness. The attention of our energy shifts from fearful to loving. We are no longer curling inward, trying to survive; we are living in trust, opportunity, expansion, & possibility. We then become models of openness to those around us, & become available to teach our children love instead of fear. Thus, we impact humanity.

Grant yourself permission to feel. Remove thought. Feel without description.

Make space for your aliveness to align itself. Let emotions flow through you as they arise. Be in acceptance. Resisting feelings keeps emotional pressure trapped in your body, & encourages more thinking, which encourages more resistance. When feelings come, remove all judgments. Cry. Let them leave. Emotions are weather systems, helping you regulate. Do not describe. Do not engage in self-loathing. Do not ask why. Provide a beautiful haven for the feelings, & stay as attentive & loving as you would with an upset child.

Notice how you choose to leave.

My primary (collective) escape tactic has been dissociation. I have 'Dissociative Identity Disorder.' Traumas in development were too much for my psyche to handle, so development was (in several instances) arrested, & separate identities were formed within the mind/body. Amnesia carefully kept us compartmentalized & seemingly functional through delegated tasks & protective measures.

We each have exhibited preferred manners of escape within the system, which have included: biting holes in the insides of my lips, tearing skin off my thumbs, obsessive compulsivity regarding cleanliness, mutism, alcohol, cigarettes, drugs, sugar, sex, cutting, running, relationships, professional sabotage, & the dramas of soliciting attention. Additionally, I have heard of many other escape tactics, including but not limited to: gambling, pornography, binge-watching television, overeating, not eating, shopping, shoplifting, cheating, gossiping, & lying. These manipulations of body & mind are all quick fixes, & employ continued self-abandonment, which catalyzes inevitable shame thereafter (unless sociopathic), keeping the inner conditioning of the false belief programming alive—*which is comprised entirely of thoughts.* Therefore, the most harmful weapon we have used against ourselves is *thinking.*

Notice what you are urged to do to avoid experiencing your emotions. Watch where your attention goes. You will begin to witness repeated narratives & questions which tend to accompany your feelings. These are the narratives & questions that keep the belief systems running, & prevent pure release of emotion.

When you feel an emotion arise—sadness, for example, pay attention to how your body feels. Where in your body do you experience discomfort? Cry from those places without thought or description. Try to relax them by breathing slowly. *You are safe.* Watch & listen to how your brain responds. As you cry (or to prevent you from crying), your brain will likely tell you what happened that made you feel sad, or who is to blame for your sadness. It might berate you for the uncomfortable tension in your stomach, throat, or heart. It might ask what's wrong with you for feeling so sad, or how someone could do what they did that resulted in your sadness. It might avoid the sadness altogether & begin devaluing or insulting your character, insisting you deserved both the event that made you sad & the sadness itself. Releasing emotion while spinning out on narratives & questions nourishes the false belief network already in place, & can actually be re-traumatizing. Alternatively, simply feeling the tension & sadness, & crying as they are experienced, is a beautifully cleansing process. The things the thoughts are about are not happening; the feelings are happening. Your consciousness has been given the casing of your body as its current vessel. Be attentive to your vessel. Be with what's actually happening. By continuing to place your attention on feeling, & discouraging accompanying thoughts, you are reconditioning your mind & learning to exist presently in your body. There is no need to escape. You are already surviving. *Live.* Live here in the flow of now's acceptance & the ever-changing possibility hereafter.

Persistent physical symptoms can guide us toward acceptance & love.

Sometimes sensory pains in our bodies are more dominant than emotional uprisings. The body will exhibit dis-ease to demand our attention. Most physical ailments & injuries I have struggled through have been psychosomatic. I was formerly severely asthmatic, & had seizure-like 'exorcisms,' during which I shook & trembled violently & uncontrollably, & felt as though I was being choked. I was embarrassed by & ashamed of these episodes. As the 'exorcisms' became more difficult to anticipate, I could no longer keep them hidden. When I moved through the haze of shame & judgment, I saw that I was simply reliving the flashback of my original trauma (& perhaps compounded energy of continued trauma I experienced thereafter). Not only did these somatic indicators lead me to exorcise the toxicity of the flashback, they disappeared once I held space for the terror to escape. The other alters have also had somatic indicators, which diminish each time they are given acute loving attention & healing is granted opportunity. The body remembers what the mind has cunningly tucked away. Trauma survivors often experience mysterious physical symptoms for which there seems to be no cure. The only medicine for these indicators of dis-ease is loving attention, as that was inevitably absent at their origins. We can grant ourselves the love we did not learn from our abusers by looking at the pain beneath these physical symptoms clearly & with compassion, & recognizing our strength in survival.

These traumas will stop inserting themselves into the present once we truly see them, remove description & judgment, feel what we felt, give ourselves love, & show ourselves we are safe now. Otherwise, they will, by design, continue our shame & suffering.

My energy & physicality were repeatedly used for power purposes by my mother. I was far too small to defend myself at first, so my body was fear-wired to freeze & stay silent as I grew. She seemed revived by these perpetrating behaviors—as though they were medicinal. Violent dominance over a child is not ever pure medicine. My mother must not have known unconditional love, acceptance, or compassion, so she consistently abandoned herself through violence & was teaching me through behavior to do the same. Her violence was directed at me, & mine was directed at myself. I did not have enough life experience or the appropriate emotional vocabulary to recognize this then. I only saw how desperately her perception of how others perceived her mattered most. Her behavior & language indicated extreme concern with how I looked (& how I therefore reflected her), & no interest in how I felt. I could make her day by being regarded as a genius by a teacher, for example, but break it by not appearing blond enough (neither of which I controlled). In my constant bewilderment, I absolutely believed that the treatment I received from her indicated my fundamental wrongness. I continued living speechlessly, keeping the poison circulating inside.

My psyche had been trying to release that toxicity from the body for years, but my mind & belief systems were trapping it into a loop. Each time the energy tried to set itself free, I was so embarrassed & ashamed that I did everything in my power to contain it. When I began to accept my seizure-like flashbacks—allowing them to exorcize the poison, allowing feelings to come through & pass, I began to heal. Those painful feelings didn't have to belong to me anymore. I realized that they never did; they belong to humanity—fright, pain, confusion, disbelief, paralysis, heartbreak. What was my mother's experience of the events? Insecurity, frustration, terror, overwhelm, rage, release, relief? What heartbreak must she have experienced to feel such shame & terror? How much pressure must she have been containing to erupt in such violent episodes? How much fear must she have felt that she could allow herself to secretly & repeatedly harm her daughter?

My alters & I each decided that the treatment we received from our mother was our fault—a common conclusion abused children draw: we deserved it. After years of living through it, & years of harming ourselves, we were able to realize that none of her behavior had anything to do with us. We simply had a front row seat to her humanity. The human experience has vast capacity. We can flow with it in acceptance, remembering our universal energetic connection; or we can become mere shadows of ourselves by interpreting unfavorable events to signify our fundamental unworthiness. We are not encouraged to glow (contrarily, we are encouraged *not* to glow) if we are raised by shadows. We must remember our pure, natural state. The universe is in balance. Every moment presents an opportunity to see clearly. Live in acceptance—accept what is & has been, then trust yourself to make choices which align with your highest self. As Aberdeen wrote in a song, 'Love is all. When all of the fighting is done, nothing has ever been wrong. Be love.'

SELF-CARE

Never has there existed a human unworthy of love.
Love yourself.

I learned in loving myself that I had chosen not to speak. It was simply a decision I made repeatedly for survival, which continued itself, impacted by fear. So, each time I found myself physically unable to speak, instead of spinning out internally with panic, I began breathing deeply, placed a hand on my heart, & looked around. I found something pleasant in my immediate surroundings—someone's quirky gesture, the boots on my feet, joy in the content of my work, the tone of a voice, the smell of coffee, a majestic tree's shade & comfort, bright flowers, clouds, small scampering creatures, the stone in my pocket… I kept stones, twigs, leaves, & sage inside my home & car for this purpose. I enjoyed their beauty. I enjoyed my silence. I chose to do something loving with & for my energy instead of resisting fear & trying to force speech. Soon enough, without urgency, I had a voice.

Feel your body.

Feel your body as something you are wearing—something you've been temporarily granted, inside which you can experience sensation & movement. Go outside. Find a tree. Stand beneath it. *Breathe slowly & deeply.* Notice your life force. Recognize that you are breathing the tree as the tree is breathing you. Notice how your breathing moves your body in a rhythm. Sway or move freely if you feel compelled. Notice the safety & trust of this circumstance. *Keep breathing slowly & deeply.* Notice temperature & breeze against your skin, how your clothing feels, any smells or sounds in the atmosphere. If thoughts try to distract you, choose to hear them without believing them. In other words, do not hate them or try to push them away; acknowledge them, but do not follow them. Bring your attention back into your body, & its relationship with the tree. *Keep breathing slowly & deeply.* This is all that is happening right now. If painful or uncomfortable physical sensations arise, you might notice fear come in, inviting further tension. Your breathing will likely quicken, as your sympathetic nervous system has been alerted to (imagined) danger, & surges of adrenalin will fire, enabling you to fight or flee. *You are safe.* Place your attention on your body sensations & breathe deeply. Intentional deep breathing reassures your body of its safety by activating the parasympathetic nervous system. Feel the sun (or the moon, stars, sky—the vastness which holds you). Feel the tree, the ground, the atmosphere. *This is all that is happening right now.* If you continue practicing this stillness (with or without a tree), you will begin to live freely wherever you are. You will not bring your past into your present. You will not bring present fears & discomforts into your future presence. You will not let your past squander your present & predict your future. Your presence will allow you to unfold a future free of knowing, & you will bring your body along for the ride.

Watch your thoughts.

Continue to recognize thought fixations & look underneath them for the feelings they help you avoid. Release the feelings, making space for something new. Replace the way you know things are with an openness to what they might be. You cannot know how anything is. You have sequestered yourself based on how things have been, but you have also been attracting these circumstances unconsciously to prove how things are, & to keep them that way. When we 'know,' we forfeit all other possibilities. Not surprisingly, this leads to depression, anxiety, vigilance, mood disorders, & addictions. How can one feel joy if one 'knows' how bad/unsafe/humiliating/terrifying/hurtful/shameful everything is destined to always be?

Your behavioral decisions & past agreements help script your thoughts, but they are not yours. You are not even doing the thinking. *You are giving audience.* How generously you pay attention (& to what) is always your choice. We operate as though our thoughts are real. They are simply frequency stations which provide clues about the perspectives from which they are broadcast. They are designed to keep us safe, but their defensive nature will continue to invite the need for defense. It is only when we drop down into the body & allow heart to influence mind, that we can experience compassion & truly see the interconnectedness. Breathe & surrender. Breathe & surrender. *Breathe. Surrender.*

Dropping into the heart is not something you force; it is something you allow.

Aberdeen will discuss this with respect to relationships, mercy, & forgiveness, as she has far more experience than I (I was mute, & therefore a spectator more than a participant), & she was the last of all of us to forgive herself...

* *

THE BRIDGE

Transitioning from suffering to freedom is a powerful, seemingly daunting & perilous endeavor. Simply, it involves learning to lead with one's heart & intuition, thereby relieving the mind of its beliefs, opinions, & thought spins. In this free state, there is nothing to hold on to. This rite of passage removes all that is not you from yourself, & you are left with nothing, which grants you everything there is. There are three phases in a rite of passage: separation, transition, & reincorporation. Picture, if you will, in transitioning from one place to the next, you are floating between them in a cosmic net bridge. If you fall out of flow in transition, the net will catch you & bounce you back into the flow, heading toward the next place. Or, you will impose familiar suffering upon yourself & return to the former place, where you may again engage in transitioning.

Separation, transition, reincorporation. Hole, bridge, light. Climb out of the hole. Brave the bridge. Embody love's illumination absolutely.

To separate from our patterns of suffering, we investigate. We discover false beliefs, trapped emotional pain, & violence in our behaviors & thoughts. In transition, we uncomfortably learn to release fear & pain, amend our minds' language, & lovingly hold space for ourselves as our behaviors, thoughts, & choices begin to shift from their conditioned habits. Ultimately, once we have crossed this cosmic bridge, when we have conditioned ourselves from judgment & resistance to compassion & acceptance, we live in expansive joy as we reincorporate our newly integrated, open, loving, expressive, aligned, fearless selves. Here, everything is undeniably a divine opportunity.

Intuition does not leave us; we choose to disregard it.

Intuition is the pull to behave—how we are compelled. True intuition only operates accurately out of good will. It favors the force & flow of life & creation. It is decision-making without the mind. It is behavior without reason. It is allowing. Rediscovering

our hearts' naked intuition grants us compassionate acceptance, & therefore, passage away from
suffering.

RELATIONSHIPS

We feel before we understand language. We learn to
interpret, anticipate, & analyze. We are trusting, sen-
sitive, vulnerable dependents. If our caretakers unload
their unresolved pain onto us (in whichever chosen
form(s) of manifested violence), secure autonomy
cannot naturally evolve. Instead, we learn fear &
survival. We become enmeshed. Our inner magnets
become energetically conditioned by twisted signals.
We tune in to someone else's frequency (forfeiting
our own), so we can appropriately anticipate danger, & behave accordingly in order to survive. That
live-wire feeling of anxiety & vigilance becomes
more acutely fine-tuned as we cross adolescence into
adulthood. It feels attracted or further ignited when
it recognizes a similarly unconscious frequency in
another being. Therefore, we rub up against energetic
reflections of ourselves.

These attractions likely elicit pleasure, relief,
panic, & familiar discomfort. We incorrectly believe
the other person is responsible for creating these pos-
itive & negative feelings within us. We can become

hooked on pleasure, which distracts us from our pain; or, we can become trapped in a cycle of blaming the other for how we feel (often in cathartic arguments), which distracts us from seeing what our projections reveal. These interactions seem to emotionally regulate us, so we often cling to them in desperation—mimicking former helpless dependence on our dysfunctional caretakers. We are trapped in our own architecture as a result of our beliefs & behaviors, which will construct traps in all aspects of our lives— perhaps most disastrously, in our relationships with ourselves & others. If we choose to look, we will see.

It's not personal; it's personal.

So, we find ourselves a 'significant other.' Whether distractingly pleasurable or sickeningly uncomfortable (or both), these entanglements allow us to feel as though we are not alone. (We are never truly alone, but we don't know that yet...) The internal energetic recognition tells us we are seen, understood, similar. All the icky secrets we each have hidden in dark places within will become apparent as intimacy grows. Even if denial is quite strong, time simply passing will invite behavioral clues which will indicate unresolved trauma (including dysfunctional developments of 'intimacy').

We attract what we subconsciously believe we deserve. We are drawn to others with similar levels of trauma, dysfunction, &/or dissociation. This allows us to enable each other's dysfunction, or it provokes us to grow. If we can recognize the other in our relationship as a mirror, & we study what's reflected, we can decide whether or not we can accept living with such self-assigned handicaps. We must look. If we look with judgment, we react with comparison, blame, righteousness, martyrdom, justification, &/or denial. If we can look without judgment, we can recondition ourselves to find the pain beneath our beliefs, thoughts, & behaviors. We can teach ourselves to hold space for ourselves kindly & gently, & grant our past pain passage from our bodies & hearts into the ether. We can see clearly that none of it means anything. We can find acceptance, compassion, & gratitude for ourselves & others. We can then clearly see that every challenging interaction in a relationship is an opportunity for growth.

So, the sensation of attraction—the magnetism, is a gift. It's an invitation to investigate. Beliefs, thoughts, & behaviors were the ego's way of protecting us. Toxic relationships, false beliefs, & dysfunctional reactive behaviors are all unsustainable without further & further denial & dissociation. Not unlike substance addiction, the aforementioned engagements work initially, but if continued, they no longer serve us; we become their slaves.

The way in which others behave toward us has nothing to do with us. How we treat others has little to do with them. It's all humanity playing itself out. The abuse we endured in development was not about us. Our significant others' projections of their own inner pain is their responsibility, not ours. We are each responsible for conducting our own level of awareness, cultivating clear perspective, & continuously choosing where we place our attention. We must be willing to look at where & how we see.

The mechanics of inner programming calculate divine orchestration.

Compulsions are patterns of attraction & tendency born from denying true curiosity. Curiosity is intuitive, & its nature is compelling—It points the way of the internal compass. When we are told as children that our natural inclinations are 'wrong,' we learn to despise our internal compass, & spend an incredible amount of energy silently strangling it into submission. We train ourselves to behave inauthentically, to adhere to what we must do for survival. We deny our curiosities in order to do what's 'acceptable' instead of accepting ourselves as we are. As we grow, in order to continue living inauthentically (& remain in survival mode), we are run solely by our inner system of compulsions. This system was so diligently & efficiently constructed that perhaps we can no longer even hear or feel our true curiosities. We 'feel' (& believe) that the compulsions are our intuition's direction, as they proudly masquerade as intuitive curiosities. They lead us into relationships in which the mirrored energy of familiar dysfunction allows us to feel found—maybe we *do* belong, maybe we *are* lovable. We remain in dysfunction as though our life depends on it, because it's what we believe love is, & we are frightened of losing it. It's Person A's fear needing love, interacting with Person B's fear needing love…or, as Seven put it earlier: shadows dancing with shadows. Each shadow is a manifestation within human capacity. Each shadow interaction is precisely placed in space & time, presenting divine opportunity for conscious evolution. All are potential catalysts for either further shadow manifestation, or acceptance, investigation, forgiveness, & awakening.

The pain we carry is exclusively accumulated abandonment of the self. If we've been programmed by fear, it is brutally painful to see (upon voluntary honest investigation) who we have been. I have been inauthentic & hurtful to people I adored & admired. I have spent decades of life energy in combat—sabotaging my experience, resisting love, fighting urges to open & express. Love is difficult to find beneath so much pain, & it certainly can't get through from the outside! I did not understand 'love'—I thought it was twisted & shallow & secretive; critical & shaming; possessive & conditional. I have suffered profoundly to guarantee my life sentence in the internal prison of my own making. I accept that this hostage situation—this self-imprisonment, was created for survival.

So…What if, with love, I look? What if I see & feel the hurt, the deep deep pain, the shame, the terror, the fear? What if I invite all the heart's requests, the ignored curiosities, the inspired imagination, the body sensations, into my space now with absolute acceptance? What if, without judgment, I can clearly see all the ways in which I abandoned myself? Can I see that I've had agency in my life all along? Is it clear that the meanings I gave to all circumstances I experienced have led me to where I am now through decision-making but are otherwise irrelevant? Can I be grateful that my particular form of survival chose fragments & amnesia & dissociation? Can I behave authentically hereafter & recognize when I've been duped again by thought or belief?

Can I forgive ALL the horrible ways in which I have compulsively hurt myself? Can I see that I am responsible for them?—that they didn't 'happen' to me? I chose to hurt myself. I chose to keep secrets; I chose not to speak. I chose to stifle curiosities. I chose to numb my mind so I didn't have to look closely at what happened to me as a child. I chose how & where I spent my time & energy. I chose to drink, smoke, cut, fuck, hide. I chose where I lived & with whom, & where I worked. I chose to behave inappropriately & get fired constantly. I chose my relationships—each friend, each lover. I chose each wound I inflicted, each excuse I hid behind, each trap I constructed, each lie I believed. I chose each time I subjugated myself to the family system, each time I behaved in accordance with someone else's fearful regulations, each time I hated myself for crying or having pain, each time I locked myself in a bathroom ashamed of my emotions, each time I fantasized about killing myself, each time I orchestrated & began a suicide attempt (but was intercepted by an alter). I chose each time I fucked for power, pleasure, &/or distraction; each time I attracted & returned to abusive men; each time I ran away from lovely men I enjoyed; each time I behaved unfaithfully. I chose each time I tore the skin off my fingers down to the bone; each time I bit holes inside my mouth; each time I cut myself because I was drowning in shame & self-hatred & the release felt like mercy; each time

I burned, trashed, or otherwise destroyed my artwork & writing; each time I sabotaged a career I'd started. I chose each time I didn't sing, each time I didn't do or say exactly what I wanted to do or say. I chose each time I went somewhere I didn't want to go, each time I stayed when I wanted to leave, each time I didn't show up.

Showing up for ourselves requires steadfast honesty & attention. We must lead with our hearts, & do & say what comes. —Yes, doing & saying what comes is what we have been doing all along; but the actions & words came from a fear-trained system, not a heart-guided space of openness. There is no judgment here; it is all contained within the divine symphony. *Forgive yourself.*

We don't get hurt emotionally; we decide we are hurt emotionally.

You cannot be emotionally hurt by someone. You cannot emotionally hurt another. You are not responsible for anyone else's emotional well-being. You are responsible for your own emotional well-being. One can behave in an emotionally abusive manner, but the recipient must agree with the perpetrator in order to be hurt (shadows dancing with shadows).

In development, when a caretaker is emotionally abusive to a child, the child doesn't understand the discomfort he/she feels, & therefore decides the behavior must mean something about him/herself in order to justify the severity of pain experienced. This is abandonment of the self & adherence to a scared scary person for survival. Later in life, that old pain can be sought out, targeted, & ignited by another. The fear & pain that get triggered (in energetic friction between you & another) are from unresolved past experiences during which you abandoned yourself. Adhering to belief systems formed around that old pain provokes unconscious behavior. When you & another abandon yourselves simultaneously (& therefore the compassion, love, & acceptance available to you in the present circumstance), you are both behaving unconsciously.

There is an intermingling of energy between you & another in any interaction, but *this is your trip.* Anyone with whom you interact helps reveal you to yourself. Your emotional well-being & ability to self-regulate are paramount. Self-regulation does not mean 'controlling' yourself & strangling your emotions into submission; it means acknowledging & releasing emotions you feel without description. When emotions are not acknowledged & released, they are trapped within us. They disturb our bodies so our attention finds them. If we continue to push emotions down, resentments & narratives accumulate in our minds which cloud our perspectives & prevent us from behaving & speaking authentically. Do not fixate your attention on someone else's behavior—you cannot control or change them, & they do not need to be controlled or changed. When fixating on another, you distract yourself from your inner experience. You pull yourself out of your body & up into your head. Your head spins obsessively & your body suffers from the neglect. This is also self-abandonment. *Tend to yourself.* Your attention is supremely valuable.

You are responsible for where you place your attention, & the perspective from which you live in each moment. You alone cause yourself suffering by not living freely from a self-regulated place of love & acceptance. If we continue to abandon ourselves, & scrutinize ourselves & others for our suffering, we are not living in love & acceptance. *We must deeply & completely forgive ourselves for all self-abandonment.* When we learn to live in our power (truth, love, light, expression), it becomes pristinely evident that others are not responsible for how we feel. We choose how we relate to ourselves & others in each moment. When we experience acceptance & love for ourselves, we experience freedom. We then have heart-space to accept others who have behaved fearfully & unconsciously toward us. Further, we find we are (surprisingly) grateful for their (unconscious, yet perfect) teachings.

Open your perspective to opportunity, presence, inclusivity, & oneness.

Truly seeing how frequently so many of us abandon ourselves evokes a deeply profound sadness. Once you see how simple it is to repeatedly do, but how much it energetically costs, the pressure of self-abandonment's debt is clear. Humanity is one entity. We collectively self-abandon. Eternal oneness must include all, so it must therefore writhe in order to learn, grow, & transform. Any war one wages on another is a war somewhere within your & my potential. Our collective potential for violence is redeemed (or at least balanced) through our collective potential for compassion. Absolute forgiveness & acceptance is allowing the mind to see through a lens only the heart (the true master of intelligence) can provide. If one's mind can humbly learn from heart's wisdom, one can employ & hold a perspective of loving attention. One then communicates in loving language inside oneself & to others. Head to heart for one is head to heart for all.

FEAR & LOVE

Our fear holds us hostage.

We believe our fear. It seems to tell us the truth. Extreme fear born in development keeps us restricted well into adulthood, as it doesn't understand the possibility of a different circumstance. It is the root of all defensive programming, & it is hardwired. It will manifest through attracting the same type of circumstance again & again, in order to prove how things 'are.' If new expansive opportunities present themselves, it will reject or sabotage them until pain has been illuminated & released, thereby altering perspective. What a clever conundrum the universe granted our analytically-minded species! Our spinning thoughts (the records we choose to keep listening to) captivate our attention. If our attention is consciously placed on love, with love, in love, for love, a story of love will unfold. Love is truth. You can't lose it.

Love is the ultimate answer.

All conflicts are made up of love. They are the direct confrontation of love battling (& being overpowered by) dark forces grown from false belief systems, which came from hurt, & we felt hurt because we loved. If we are compelled to look closely enough, we will find love at the center of every conflict—desire for connection, longing for acceptance, the openness truth invites, the opportunity for forgiveness. These concepts do not seem possible in practice, as they are shielded by fear. We become ornery, distant, cold, skeptical, paranoid, possessive, unkind, comparative, demeaning, envious, cruel, violent, judgmental, self-righteous, controlling, depressed, isolated…all because of what we are scared of & believe we don't have—that which we actually ultimately cannot lose: LOVE. Love *IS*. We are frightened of our capacity. The inner knowing of love will shine through on its own unless it is constantly cloaked in darkness, which is why these false beliefs must consistently find creative ways to prove themselves. Those of us who have survived trauma energetically attract relationships & circumstances to recreate the 'truths' of our false belief systems. We often recognize that there is a pattern, or at least a feeling of repetition, but we feel lost & do not know why. This confusion & alienation conveniently feed into the false belief loop system.

False beliefs deny us the love, connection, & acceptance we desire by deciding, convincing, & then repeatedly proving to us that we don't deserve love or are not worthy of love. We thus believe, falsely, that love is conditional & limited rather than free & abundant. We started believing mistruths about ourselves & the world when our hearts were broken. When we were rattled with pain & fear as children, we came up with reasons for other people's unconscious behavior toward us. We found the reasons within ourselves—it was our fault. We are damaged, flawed, stupid, ugly, evil, worthless. We chose these false beliefs in order to survive, in order to justify the hell we lived through. Then, we continue through life 'knowing' how irreversibly damaged, flawed, stupid, ugly, evil, & worthless we are. No amount of evidence to the contrary can change our minds because we are still living in fear. Our fears drew conclusions, & we agreed. Our souls (the divine oneness within us unencumbered by thought, belief, reason, or circumstance) will send signals to us through somatic responses, physical ailments, compulsions, & mental disorders, that we are misaligned. Fear & resistance prevent us from experiencing freedom & joy. Truth & acceptance are demanding our attention! No child has ever been born damaged, flawed, stupid, ugly, evil, or worthless. It is up to us to investigate the authenticity of our beliefs with deliberate compassion. Through honest investigation, we will only ever find love at the center of our swirling fears & rigid pain. Further, there is nothing we need to believe. What is *is*—it needs no legitimization.

Love to a traumatized adult or child can feel extremely frightening. To me, it has often felt like a trick. Trust. (...*How?!?!*) Once you have forgiven yourself for all self-abandonment, you have made space to trust yourself moving forward in authenticity, & you have made it impossible to fall into an inauthentic space without discovering you decided to leave truth & presence for conclusions & beliefs. Trust yourself to listen inwardly, to behave & speak in truth, & to acknowledge your feelings of fear as they are simmering. Continue to investigate your beliefs as they pull at your attention. Continue reminding yourself to love.

From a false belief's point of origin comes attention placement & perspective.

Since beliefs cultivate perspective, we must return to the original seeds of our beliefs in order to uproot them & create opportunity for a clear, truthful perspective. The path there is not through thought. In order to justify an abusive upbringing (& survive it), we mangled our minds into suspicion & vigilance, & from this negative perspective we keep looking & thinking to figure it all out. It is not surprising, then, that we continue to form & believe negative conclusions. We repeatedly place our attention wherever our darkened perspectives indicate. We look at what we have decided is wrong with us & what we don't have. We allow further limitations our perceived deficiencies inspire to be true as well, thereby limiting our behaviors & choices, & keeping us resistant. We feel as though we are trapped. *We do this to ourselves.* We must discover & recognize where we are placing our attention, then choose to place it instead on love. Be grateful for the opportunity to learn & evolve. Again, once we have truly forgiven ourselves for abandoning ourselves—which includes our false belief constructions & adherence to them, we can trust ourselves to behave authentically, which is, in essence, trusting our participation in life.

You cannot heal pain with your thoughts.

Giving meaning to a happening is believing your perspective's story. The meaning is not what happened, & it's not real anyway because the memory is no longer happening. All suffering comes from our attachments to what things mean, &/or how they ought to be different than what they are. Dropping descriptions & expectations is immediately effective, as in doing so, you will realize that meaning doesn't matter. All the weighted mattering you have given to life events & interactions with others can evaporate. Remove the story.

You might feel angry, for example, & that anger might seem directed toward a particular person, but if you remove the thoughts & stories fueling the anger, you are simply left with a feeling in your body. Go for a run, scream into a pillow, hit a drum, sing loudly, chant, take up boxing, lie down & do tension exercises isolating specific muscles in your body from head to toes. Stay with the feeling, do not get lured in by what your mind has to say about it.

Perhaps, in another instance, you feel desperately sad. Recognize first how old this pain is. Tremendously intense feelings are those which have accumulated their tension over time, as they have not been properly addressed. Sit with the sadness. Let it breathe. You have likely been choking it down in self-judgment. Your current sadness doesn't mean anything, nor does your former reluctance to experience it. Nothing is supposed to be any other way than it is right now. *Cry.* Place your hands on your heart. Be kind to yourself. Show yourself you are safe. Breathe deeply. Do not entertain combative thoughts. Stay focused on your body—your breathing, your hands, your heart. *Be gentle.* Watch how your body responds as you treat it lovingly.

Living is experiential. Be alive without interpretation. Do not allow your attention to be bullied & subjugated by your thoughts. Find yourself in the spaces between your thoughts, & continue choosing to place your attention on gratitude & love. Further, gratitude for these precise moments of recognition & course correction during episodes of suffering will deepen exponentially as you practice. Eventually, gratitude & acceptance will become your consistent state of being, & you will no longer experience suffering.

Emotional discomfort is impermanent.

Feelings will release if you allow their passage. It may seem as though an episode of discomfort will never end. That thought indicates fear & resistance, which will encourage the emotion(s) to linger & perhaps worsen in severity. Accept the discomfort with clarity & gentleness, & let it leave you. Familiar suffering repeats itself only because you continue choosing to invite it. So, stop & listen to your body when your head is spinning, or when you feel emotions rising. Don't get lured away by your thoughts—judgments, opinions, memory, imagination. Recognize your true awareness witnessing the thinking. Keep your attention on your heart, your breathing, & any sensations that arise. Release your pain with love (which is usually in the form of tears), & please don't judge yourself or your pain as it leaves. Demonstrate kindness. *Teach yourself unconditional love.* Make a ritual of it! Set aside time every morning &/or evening to sit quietly for even a few moments, finding sensations & accepting them, releasing any pain that presents itself, & consciously experiencing love for yourself.

Discomfort that lives in you will inevitably come to greet you. You cannot lose the truth of what is, but you can get rid of everything else. In fact, all things untrue want to leave, & your resistance to their departure is what makes you miserable. Look at your perspectives without agreeing with them. Be diligent with your commitment to self-compassion. Judgment is no longer welcome, nor are ill-fated conclusions. You will notice where you tend to place your attention, & which thoughts & behaviors you allow yourself to repeat. This will lead you to discover your false beliefs, providing opportunity for dismantling, & evolution. Can you be grateful for whatever you find, & the opportunity to heal yourself by releasing your pain? Can you commit to loving all the fear protecting you from living in love?

THE VORTEX OF
GENERATIONAL TRAUMA

We trick ourselves in order to survive.

We absorbed the energy of what our caretakers expressed toward & around us. We also felt what they were suppressing. All energy in this vortex is carried forward, as all behavior is communication, in a contained circus of existence manifestation. Our minds are constantly collecting data & tending to puzzles of input by attaching meaning to circumstance. Our hearts are like antennae—receptors of energy. What is felt & observed behaviorally works together with language to effectively carry inner violence, shame, & unhealthy perspectives forward. Our preoccupation with & adherence to this conditioned dysfunctional programming comprises the unconscious outfit which keeps us from being led by our naked heart's navigation.

Please recall, for a moment, that I have Dissociative Identity Disorder. When we (in this body) were beginning to successfully work with co-consciousness (the ability to see & hear what other alters were doing & saying while in front), Leaha (the body's 'host,' in psychological categorization) was teaching therapeutic yoga for trauma in a mental health care facility. The yoga sessions involved some gentle physical asana practice for grounding, then a group discussion. This format was not intentional; it evolved this way. One of the patients would ask a question, then within Leaha's answer, a topic would present itself. Sometimes I recorded audio on my phone to listen clearly later, as I was suffering tremendously & was baffled that my brain & her brain (*the same brain*) could have such wildly different opinions & perspectives...

One day, a patient shared that he was sometimes able to feel 'happy or even just ok', but it 'never lasts' because he 'returns to reality'—in which he feels miserable & experiences suffering. I shared his predicament!—Each time I fell back out of vibrant expansive spaces in experience, I felt tricked & defeated & 'knew' that the darkness was my natural state. Leaha responded to this fellow by inviting the group to open to the possibility that *our natural state is presence,* & that suffering occurs when we leave presence & live in our minds, which are likely replaying & analyzing the past, or anxiously imagining future circumstances. So, could this patient be open to the possibility that he does not get 'tricked' into presence & then dumped back into reality? Instead: is it possible that he fleetingly experiences presence—which is his true nature, & then fear &

conditioning & thoughts trick him back into believing that suffering is his reality? I didn't buy it. In fact, it angered me. It seemed to anger the patient as well. He 'knows it's true' that he suffers, he said. Leaha replied, 'Yes. You experience suffering. It is awful & painful & continuous. I am not invalidating you. I hear you, & want your suffering to end! I want you to spend more time living & less time thinking. Presence! I am proposing there's more to your experience, potentially, than what you think & believe.'

That day at the treatment center, Leaha disclosed her own diagnosis (DID), & confessed that she had often felt shame & embarrassment around her confusion when she would come back to the front after having been blacked out by amnesia, & questioned by those closest to her. She did not have answers & she often found herself having to clean up some physical, emotional, sexual, professional, or energetic mess I (or another alter) had made in her absence. She had been preoccupied with what had happened, why she couldn't remember, when something similarly bewildering would happen again, & how she could make the blackouts & unexplainable behavior stop. In doing so, she was living in her head & suffering, preventing herself from presence in the time she had available to be present! She decided to live in acceptance. She decided she could be ok with what she knew & didn't know. She didn't have to fear what was coming. Anxiety would only exacerbate the condition & the confusion surrounding it. 'So let's be here, where we are, while we're here, & see what happens.'

This discussion of presence, acceptance, & being in experience instead of thought provoked the patients to recognize that they did, in fact, spend most (if not all) of their time swimming around (& often drowning) in their thoughts. Although no patient in the room had DID, & no two patients in the room had the same diagnosis/affliction, they were all connected in this way. Their suffering came from their belief systems which informed their conditioned thought patterns.

Granted, Leaha had an easier time surrendering to acceptance, as the whole structure of DID kept her protected from the traumas we had experienced in her body, so she therefore did not experience our trauma flashbacks. We each absorbed our delegated genres of imposed pain & violation. Fragmenting was a coping mechanism, & each fragment developed individual perspectives, based on unique belief systems, based on fear & pain that had not been metabolized. *We did not feel safe.* Our thoughts proved to us that we were not safe by reliving, imagining, detecting, attracting, & inviting danger.

I saw how my thoughts attempted to protect me. I traced patterns & beliefs back to family conditioning, & saw that I had indeed tricked myself in order to survive. By believing I was 'evil, stupid, ugly, & wrong,' for instance, I *deserved* the shaming, criticism, & brutality I received. These 'true' flaws were irredeemable, & therefore being punished harshly for these 'truths' tracked. By believing these 'truths,' I fit into the family system & allowed its dysfunction to seem appropriate. By carrying these beliefs forward into adulthood with me, I shunned or sabotaged people & situations that challenged them, & I invited people & situations into my life that would help me reinforce them (shadows dancing with shadows).

I came to believe my body & emotions betrayed me when they were actually screaming for my attention. Presence does not trick us away from a dark reality of endless thought; presence is light & truth. We hide & trick ourselves away from truth. We surrender our clear sight in order to exist within our family of origin's dysfunction. We then, unknowingly, become perfect carriers of dysfunctional behavior & perspective.

Past blood has led you to this moment, but you can alter this blind fate if you are willing. Observe your thoughts & behaviors. You can condition yourself out of habits you've conditioned yourself into! By acknowledging your thoughts & behaviors, holding loving space for the pain beneath them, & embodying gratitude, you can defeat darkness with light.

Observe your language & behaviors.

In observing your language & behaviors, you will illuminate the medicine(s) you have chosen to regulate your emotions. If honesty, compassion, & acceptance are employed, you will be able to discern whether these choice medicines are nourishing or harmful. From there, you can decide to influence those choices with love, thereby interrupting your habitual cycles of conditioning. Incorporating meditation (sitting quietly, focusing your attention on your breathing, & simply witnessing your body & mind) is incredibly helpful in the transition from harmful self-regulation to loving acceptance & peace.

Here are some questions to consider (*Please visit this book's Appendix for a more thorough guided self-investigation.*): How do you use language when speaking to others? What is the familiar language of your thoughts? Do you nourish your body lovingly? Do you harm your body? Are you critical or accepting of your physical self? Are you honest with yourself & others? How do you experience intimacy (or do you avoid it)? Are you able to rest & sleep well?

Do you often experience physical symptoms of discomfort? What secrets are you holding in reverence?

Do not judge yourself. Nothing is wrong. Just look & feel & listen.

Breathe deeply. In this moment, drop all labels. Do not define yourself or others. Do not describe, defend, rationalize, justify, or identify. Identifications are traps. Believing in descriptions may initially provide security, but it is ultimately extremely limiting. Labels are conclusive & do not invite change. For example, you might be experiencing anger, timidness, or depression; but declaring that you are an 'angry,' 'shy,' or 'depressed' person negates the nature of impermanence, therefore perpetuating cycles of the very characteristics or moods you could otherwise be moving through. As you observe inauthenticity in your language & behavior, you will likely be able to see how confining, repetitive, & predictable your particular styles of self abandonment are. Can you see that you've been lying to yourself & others? It's ok! You configured these games to survive...& you survived. *You're alive.* Breathe. Observe this beautiful opportunity for change. You can now expand your experience of being alive from mere survival to vibrant aliveness.

We are infinite. Within each of us lives all the potential of humanity. You don't know what you might do today if you open to the possibility of change. Accept everything in your life right now as it is, then decide what you want & don't want on your trip. Then: What might you want to invite? *This is your trip.* Everyone else is on their own trip. We are catalysts for each others' growth—one living being, living & being.

Vow to honor your feelings & intuition. You will surprise yourself with new behavior. Choose to open your perspective, & watch yourself become a more loving, accepting, forgiving, spontaneous being. When you find yourself behaving in a more consistently loving manner, you will not need to label yourself; along the way to becoming consistently loving, you will shed the insecurities which seek comfort in identification.

Please use loving language.

Reprogramming requires exorcising the painful emotions wound tightly around our hearts, clogging our physical bodies & energetic flow. We must also change the way we communicate with ourselves & others. These evolutions happen synchronously.

You are a survivor on the grand spectrum of generational trauma. Family dysfunction is a swirling system of secrets. Hold space for your secrets & release the pain beneath them from your being. Remove description & meaning from the circumstances. The stories around the secrets, the beliefs you created in surviving them, & the trapped pain you felt in experiencing them keep you from presence & feed your suffering. You have an inner dialogue with these secrets. They have a vampiric, manipulative, demeaning, threatening language. This language was learned & encouraged through fear & unconscious conditioning within your family system. It now lives in you. (*Remove judgment. Nothing is wrong. Just look.*) Although the secrets may still be kept, their language is assertive & unruly. It explodes in physical violence, rage, blaming, shaming, criticizing, superiority, & condescension. It implodes in all manner of active self-destruction (addiction, self-harm, self-hatred, sabotage, negative thoughts). *This is all violence.*

Start speaking to yourself & others differently.

Words were created to convey, describe, connect. If you are using words which align with an ashamed, frightened, judgmental perspective, your program is continually reinforcing itself. Drop 'should' & 'supposed to.' Choose what you are doing or not doing. *You decide.* Drop asking 'why' others behave as they do. Instead, look into yourself & address how you feel, without description. Then, decide what comes next in the next present moments as the moments present. Drop being conclusive by dropping 'always' & 'never.' Drop negative fearful words such as 'hate' & 'can't.' There is anger beneath 'hate.' Find the anger in your body, acknowledge it, breathe into it, & let it go consciously through vocal expression or physical activity. There is resignation beneath 'can't.' Find the feelings that encourage this self-abandonment & let them go consciously through crying or physical movement. Drop 'have to' & 'need to;' urgency is poison. Drop 'I'm serious' when you want to be heard—try instead: 'I'm being sincere.' You will feel whether or not you are in fact speaking with sincerity. Seriousness implies strategy, heaviness, & a lack of play. Spontaneity's vitality is purely sincere; it is not manipulative or serious. Say 'Thank you' sincerely. Answer 'How are you?' sincerely. You can do this even if you are struggling. Keep coming from a place of acceptance. Accept your struggle. Be grateful for what your particular suffering allows you to uncover. Nothing is wrong. Stop the flow of your attention's energy toward perceived problems & deficiencies, & place your thoughts & dialogue instead on gratitude & opportunity.

Shift all thoughts from a trapped perspective to an expansive perspective. For example, instead of: 'I want to quit smoking but I can't,' use these words: 'I choose to breathe clean air deeply.' The former instigates shame & demonstrates an unwillingness to change; the latter is inspiring & beautifully empowering. Another example might be: 'I know this relationship is toxic & I want to leave, but what if I can't find another man/woman who will love me(?), & how will I find a new place to live(?), & maybe this isn't really that bad(?!!?).' Instead: 'I intuitively feel compelled to leave this relationship & spend some time on my own right now. I am reclaiming my own energy & space. I trust I will find what comes next. I'm grateful for what this relationship has taught me.' Shift your attention *now*. In this moment, *decide* to bring presence, acceptance, opportunity, inclusivity, expansiveness, & positivity to all thought & conversation you encounter within yourself & with others. Gratitude will increase within you exponentially. There is, in any moment, so much to be grateful for. Gratitude is awe-inspiring. Surrender to & thank everything that seems 'wrong.'

Employ gratitude & keep returning to it.

Notice when your thoughts are negative, & negative language is being used. Notice your tone. Notice you are in the dysfunctional programming, living on the data obtained from past self-manipulated experience. Instead, right in the moment of your noticing, appreciate what's around you. Want what you have. Start primitively. Be thankful you exist! Be thankful for breathing, for clean water, for shelter, for nature's composition wherever you are, for clothing, for this body that has wandered with you through life. Notice these incredible gifts! Get specific—maybe you're grateful for the pinecones you recently collected, the food you have just prepared for yourself, the particular face your pet or child just made, the job you have that pays for your home, the clothing you have to keep you warm, the body you wear that communicates with you so clearly when you choose to listen. *You are alive! You are experiencing aliveness!* Watch your life, & acknowledge what you do & have with humility. That elicits gratitude. If you can't find gratitude easily, make it a mission. Perhaps you are grateful for reading this book at this exact moment, for your curiosity, for your desire to heal yourself from the choking grip of old wounds.

COME HOME

We were brought into our family's home. Now we make our own homes & families.

The perspectives, questions, observations, & practices in this book may indeed apply to anyone who wishes to live more freely & authentically. They may help anyone who has survived any type of trauma at any stage of life. The effects of generational trauma bleed out into the human population & intermingle, thereby igniting new traumas, which then carry themselves (if left unresolved) through their respective lineages. I am most deeply compelled to reach women whose minds & hearts have been twisted by beliefs they formed in development, in reaction to their mothers' unconsciousness. The maternal force, when pure & unobstructed, is an incredibly beautiful vibrant light of nurturing energy.

I grew up frightened every day that I would be physically hurt, shamed, &/or criticized for reasons I could not track or understand. I have felt so much hatred toward myself. I've seen so many women restrain their own vitality because they had learned to do so for survival. Fear was modeled for us in whatever manifestations our mothers expressed it. We are grown bonded with our mothers' energetic calibration. If their will to live led them to stifle their lives in order to survive their upbringings (& they did not investigate this pain), our will to live then leads us to stifle our lives to survive their unconscious mothering.

Our mothers deliver us from ether to our birthdate. We transition inside our mothers' bodies. We feel mother's frequency; we are tuned in to her station. Mothers are our primary teachers of life—we learn energies, tones, & sensations in the womb. Once we emerge, we begin the subconscious analytical journey of deciding to correlate how well our mothers respond to our needs with how deserving we are or are not to have those needs met. We watch our mothers behave. We see & feel how they interact with us, & how they interact with our fathers, other humans, animals, & objects. We see & feel how they perceive & treat themselves.

Our parents (or parental figures) ideally demonstrate to us through behavior & language that we are loved, & that it is safe for us to grow & coexist freely. If our parents do not know how to love themselves (or each other) unconditionally, & do not allow themselves (or each other) to grow & coexist freely, they cannot create an ideal environment for their children. Our parents were likely existing on the same frequency of consciousness around the time of our conception, as the divinity of the universe plays match-maker just so. If you are born to a violent mother who is unable to self-regulate, for example, it is likely that your father is equally as unconscious in his choice manifestation(s). Perhaps he drinks, overworks, gambles, cheats, or otherwise dissociates. They encourage each other's denial in order to remain in their established relationship. Your birth gave your parents a massive opportunity to investigate, & use light to evolve through their darkness (individually & together). It has always been up to them to look truthfully at themselves & each other…or not. You're in their circus for a while. Then it becomes your opportunity & responsibility to look truthfully at yourself.

If we don't investigate our unhealthy behaviors, we continue to attract or remain locked in 'intimate' alienating relationships with others who also communicate through fear & have abandoned their hearts. When we procreate unconsciously in these dysfunctional relationships, we pass the torch of fear & denial along to our offspring, who will either: continue the lineage of suffering in their personalized manifestation(s); or, recognize the dysfunction & commit to blasting it with love, thereby altering the swirling pull of the vortex.

'Home' is the system's headquarters.

In a dysfunctional family, 'home' is where violence happened, where secrets were kept, where emotions were stifled, where hearts were neglected. The word (& concept of) 'home' is therefore associated with discomfort & dysfunction. When we find we are home in ourselves, in our bodies, in love & acceptance, in oneness, 'home' is no longer a trap we might find ourselves in; it's an inner acknowledgment of freedom. When we nurture ourselves repeatedly through pain with love & mercy, we neurologically reinforce the true home we are finding within ourselves. This home is life, vitality, acceptance, belonging. We are home in every moment. From this home, we can nurture abundantly.

Humanity will be strengthened by conscious mothering. If we can create a safe space for our families to be who they are, not who they need to pretend to be to survive our unconscious fears & insecurities, we will inspire a contagion of openness & acceptance for future generations. We must first heal ourselves in truth & love. When we know we are home in every moment, we cannot impose or entertain separateness, isolation, or insecurity.

We (the dissociated identities within me) are independent perspective fragments, which hold separate emotional content from past disturbances. Our compartmentalized collections of beliefs were born of trauma, & we identified with them. These beliefs defined us to ourselves, & we each agreed respectively. We are all me. I am one of several fragments within the body, but I am no more separate from them or the body than the body is from humanity, or a wave is from the ocean. If we are labeled by others (smart, funny, ugly, skinny, fat, charming, reliable, bothersome, etc), & we agree with such label(s), we become a person who identifies as such. If we decide through maltreatment that we are dumb, ugly, worthless, dysfunctional, off-putting, unworthy of love, etc., we construct a person who fits those descriptions. But identification can only take place in the mind. Anything we learn about ourselves is completely futile, as we are not separate from the world in which we live. We are not separate from our home. We became separated from our true home when, within the walls of the homes in which we lived as children, the construct of being a separate person was scared into us, & we began adhering to who or what this particular person is or ought to be.

'What's wrong with you?'

Nothing. Absolutely nothing is *wrong* with anyone. 'Wrong' is a judgment. We might hear that question frequently from an unconscious parent as she is being reflected by you in a way that makes her uncomfortable. It's her inner pain that's being triggered by your presence, so it feels 'wrong' within her. As children, we idolize our parents, & believe they know things we don't, so we believe after much repetition of this question, that there must indeed be something 'wrong' with us. We carry this question internally, feeling ashamed of ourselves & constantly looking. Our over-active survival-mode brains find a myriad of wrongs & obsess over them, never being competent enough (it seems) to find them all, figure them out, or fix them. These are painful distractions. The appropriate question is: 'How do you feel?' Ashamed? Angry? Frustrated? Depressed? Lonely? Frightened? ...Perfect! Feel whatever it is & let your body release it. *Nothing is wrong with you, & nothing is wrong.* Nothing has ever been wrong.

We have identified ourselves inaccurately.

We have been wrapped up in an apparent identity of ourselves, constructed for survival, based on what other people reinforced to us about ourselves in development. (We are like this & not like that. We excel at this, but not at that. We look or dress like this, but not like that. We like this, but don't like that.) We were exploited, so we remain in secrecy, adhering to a construct, fearing further exploitation. Identifications can severely limit & divide us. This endless categorizing & compartmentalizing is comparative, hierarchical, unconscious, false-belief-driven programming. It keeps us from experiencing ourselves & each other. It imprisons us in shame. We are so ashamed that we ultimately identify ourselves to ourselves as separate, & no amount of external identification can reassure us we belong, as the programming we were taught (& agreed with) was designed by others who also could not find their belonging, their sameness. Our pain, in its secrecy, feels unique & monstrous. Living in adherence to our minds, we move further & further away from the ever-present abundant opportunity for connection. We accumulate more pain, & must use more energy to drown out its yearning to be seen, heard, felt, & released.

There formerly existed within me a necessary cycle of self-abuse which would covertly follow authentic expression or true feelings of aliveness. I was a slave to my thoughts, which ordered me to punish myself for behaving in any type of spontaneous expansive manner. Beholden to old fear & false beliefs, I complied.

My suicide attempts had not been successful, as other alters intervened to protect themselves & the whole being. (They collectively wanted to 'kill Aberdeen' so they could feel safe (I was quite destructive & reckless), but that obviously wouldn't work out in their favor...) Suicidal ideation was a logical response. I didn't want to live because I wasn't here—I felt I was already dead. I had already chosen to agree with inauthentic programming for survival; I had already suicided to survive. I spent my energy preventing the flow of intuitive behavior, or profoundly perpetrating myself for daring to be free. This war required all of my energy. I was often so overwhelmed with pain & dysfunction & insecurity, that suiciding— taking my life away, dying, vanishing, ending—somehow seemed a noble move. I wanted to again save myself from my life experience. Fortunately, there is a far more noble death of self, which yields aliveness, abundant vitality, & undeniable freedom.

Truth lives in behavior & feeling—in experience without thought. Truth is not in thought. It is true that your mind generates thoughts, but the thoughts themselves (descriptions, narratives, analysis, identity, constructs) are not true. Those thoughts are happening about something that's not happening now. They don't mean anything. If you choose to drop everything other than acceptance, you will see everything & everyone (including yourself) where they're at. You will recognize authenticity, & you will recognize the fear & pain behind inauthenticity. Look honestly at any anger, frustration, or sadness that arises. Let those emotions pass through you. Release them from your body. Empathy & compassion were hidden beneath them all along.

Who we think we are & who we think we ought to be must die in order for us to live. The programs in our minds must stop living through us, for us. We must stop obeying their commands, & we must stop believing them.

Grant your shame mercy.

No plant, nor animal, nor insect, nor cloud, nor stone has compared itself to another or lived in judgment & self-imposed suffering. Humanity is of nature. We are of humanity. We are *alive.* Our minds have been keeping us from accepting this perfection, made up of countless perceived 'imperfections.'

I uncomfortably surrendered repeatedly to all the anger & sadness beneath my heartbreaking shame, & found mercy. Mercy carried me further toward love & truth each time I chose its grace over shame's hypnotic familiarity. I became grateful for everything that had transpired in my experience of life— grateful for the pain, grateful for all my choices, grateful for the recognition that I have always been choosing, grateful for the choice to stop giving faithful audience & agreement to self-abusing thoughts, grateful I could choose to end suffering. Mercy had always seemed to me a blessing granted to those who deserved it, & I certainly did not assume I qualified. I chose mercy from the inside as I showed myself what love is. I slowly stopped inflicting self-harm by employing compassion instead of judgment as it happened. We must brave the distance across the bridge from suffering to ultimate recognition of our own divinity. We must trust we are each & altogether everything in the universe. We must trust that nothing is wrong.

Our present circumstance serves our highest interest.

Our divine perfection is ever-changing. Everything that we have ever experienced is perfect. Every interaction with every relative, every acquaintance, every authority, every child, every friend, every lover… is perfect. Every circumstance we have witnessed or participated in—every tragedy, every comedy, every failure, every achievement, every job, every relationship, every marriage, every divorce, the birth of every child…is perfect. However long we spend submerged in suffering is perfect. Every awakening is perfect. Every choice has been perfect, as every moment has offered a divine opportunity to choose the next divine opportunity. These opportunities might ultimately wake us to the divineness of clearly seeing that everything is one thing manifesting itself. We are all the same living being, living & being. We continue to participate divinely (whether we know it or not) by choosing (whether we know it or not) whatever we want.

If the state of our inner experience is fixated on thoughts, ideas, fear, & survival, we cannot be present & open to opportunity. Fine-tuning our compassion & attention placement breeds clear awareness—consciousness in being. 'Knowing,' then, clearly becomes feeling without thought. There are no answers, as there are no questions. There are no questions, as there are no problems. There are no decisions, as there is only intuitive knowing. Curiosity continues divine presence as intuition navigates. No amount of analysis is necessary for intuition to navigate divinely. There is no story; there is simply the spontaneity of what we decide without thought.

To end suffering, we must be willing to feel pain. Our quick-fix escape tactics (vices) are easy & available—most are even encouraged through media... but they don't require courage. Many of us choose familiar suffering over looking at what we don't want to see. Our familiar suffering seems far less difficult than feeling the pain necessary to move through it.

Observe humanity clearly without judgment.

Trends in kindness (love), & cruelty (fear) are evident on a global level, & accurately reflect where our species places its loving or fearful attention. Polarities are difficult to accept; we want to invite & hold on to the good, & admonish & avoid the ugly, & we have conflicting opinions & practices within our species regarding morality. If we grew up in dysfunction, unconscious practices were modeled for us by our caretakers. Evidence of these hidden dark places has spread through families, communities, cultures, nations, & ultimately, throughout the planet. If we can courageously nurture ourselves with love, we can cultivate more loving circumstances, & heal from fear. Living in love, truthfulness, acceptance, & compassion is the most profound gift we can give ourselves, & the highest service we can provide for humanity.

It all goes together like this.

The universe holds infinite space. Trusting this net grants us freedom from feeling caught in it. Open. Become vulnerable. Experience what you will experience. You contribute constantly to the balance of everything contained. Your particularities all belong here within you exactly as you are. We are all making choices. We all fit together as we are, doing exactly what we're doing right now. We cling to our beliefs for survival just as tightly as they cling to us when we begin to suspect their dishonesty. As we see more clearly, the patterns of our choices change. The opportunity of awareness is humanity's salvation.

This is all divine.

All orchestration is designed to bring us home to love & oneness. Love is all around us, ever-available. Everything is made of love. Fear, its opposition, was born of pain. We feel pain because we love. Therefore, fear is also born of love. We leave love. We *choose* to leave love. We protect ourselves because we are afraid of pain. We are all born made of love, with the capacity to know & live love. Our hearts were wounded by hearts that were wounded by hearts that were wounded. Our brains were programmed to keep us alive. Love appears to have abandoned us, but it peeks through in spite of our best efforts to convince ourselves of its absence. We are forever dealing & trading hands in the currency of love, hurting others so we don't get hurt, manipulating others so we can outsmart love, simulating love to get more love. These compulsions are divine trickery for our curiosity to discover. There is no limit to love. There is no way to divide love. We are all composed of love. We forget. We simply must remember.

Find your heart & let it heal you.

Let us rid ourselves of judgment, superior & inferior posturing, isolation & feigned weakness, comparisons & competition, ridicule & scorn, threats & shaming, inauthenticity & secrets. Let us come together as we already are—in oneness, & shine through all the pain together, in courage, truth, accountability, & love. Let us show our little ones that emotions are not shameful inadequacies; they are powerful healing tools. Let our modeling of vulnerability encourage our little ones to stay attuned to their hearts, & not be so easily led astray by their minds & the constructs set up to compare, describe, & separate. Let us demonstrate truth in our word & authenticity in our behavior, & they will see, learn, emulate, & experience freedom. Let us teach them how to hold space, instead of contaminating it so that they learn to be swallowed by it. Let us teach them they are worthy of love, light, life, expression, & any curiosity that intrigues them. Let us teach them the ground & encourage them to fly, all while loving ourselves & truly seeing, hearing, & honoring each other in presence. Let us be grateful for the privilege of life, & inspire conscious behavior for future generations.

You are love. Decide to see truth in presence. Start now. Every moment is a beginning, an opportunity, a new place from which you can clearly see & embody acceptance & love. Let your heart show you what comes next.

I am grateful for you & I love you.

* * * * * * * * * * * * * * ** * * * * * * * *

Appendix:
Compassionate Self-Investigation

Please incorporate a meditation practice as you work through this self-investigation. Sit quietly, close your eyes, & breathe. Acknowledge anything & everything you feel. With each inhale, nourish your body. With each exhale, release what you no longer need. Accept. Love. Heal. Witness your thought contributions, but do not entertain their messages.

Please take your time with this. Do not overwhelm yourself. Consider the suggestions below, & answer the posed questions as truthfully as you can. Accept the answers you find without judgment. Accept any discomfort that arises. Accept any emotions that stir. Continue to give yourself love. *Nothing is wrong.*

Let pain leave your body. Please do not continue to hold it in with force & shame, & please do not criticize or judge it as it leaves. Let yourself cry if/when you feel compelled to cry, & let that crying simply be crying without description. Thank yourself for thinking

& behaving as you have *in order to survive.* As you practice developing a more compassionate relationship with yourself & your life experience, any inauthentic or pain-inducing behaviors you discover will change.

Please use the blank page spaces between each collection of questions (if you wish) for sketches, musings, or discoveries you encounter. Please also acknowledge these spaces between sections as reminders to pause, breathe, & be gentle. There is no urgency in flow & acceptance. Do not rush through your feelings to get what you think completing the work might award you. There is nothing else to find & nowhere else to be. Be absolutely here, where you are. Look & you will see...

Please begin with a meditation, during which you slow your breathing down, connect with your body, thank yourself for all manner of survival tactics employed from birth until now, & vow to practice unconditional love & acceptance as you witness your behavior. Ask to see. You are looking. You are choosing to look...

Observations in Meditation

Observe your mind's language.

Observe the tone in which you deliver language. How do you speak to each person you encounter? Observe words you use frequently. Are they competitive? Comparative? Critical? Judgmental? Shaming? Self-deprecating? Condemning? Sarcastic? Defensive? Do you yell or interrupt? Do you diminish your voice & stay silent when you wish to speak?

...What might patience, kindness, acceptance, & compassion feel like in all branches of your communication?

Observations

Do you say what you want? What you need? How you feel? (Can you connect with what you want/need/feel?) Are you honest? *Just look.* Are you manipulative to elicit a favorable or avoidant response? Do you lie about your behaviors to justify & minimize them? Do you embellish your achievements to impress others?

…What might it feel like if everything you want, need, & feel is ok? What if everything you are & everything you have done is perfect? In this moment, can you forgive everything you've done & said to hurt yourself &/or others, & employ compassion, honesty, & acceptance? Can you recognize that hurtful behaviors & words are manifestations of insecurity, & that you belong here exactly as you are?

Observations

Observe the central characters in your current life experience. Do you enjoy these people? Do you feel uncomfortable around any or all of these people? Do you continue to endure interactions instead of speaking truthfully or ending relationships? Do you talk negatively about people to other people?

…What might it feel like to treasure everyone who enters your life, & trust yourself to keep them close or let them go? Can you incorporate compassion into your relationships & interactions? 'Compassionate' does not mean 'nice.' Compassion is the recognition of & concern for suffering & can therefore help alleviate suffering. Through a compassionate perspective, you will clearly recognize the pain behind violent language & behavior. Self-compassion teaches us to care for ourselves from our hearts—to remove judgment & behave intuitively. When we care for ourselves compassionately, we care for others by default & by divine design. What might it feel like to value your time & energy so deeply that you honor your heart & intuition in all circumstances, thereby honoring the evolution of humanity?

Observations

Observe the language in your head. How do your thoughts speak to you? What do your thoughts say to you about yourself? What do they say about others? Observe the perspectives from which the language comes. Can you find the fear & insecurity? *Just look. Nothing is wrong.* Can you recognize judgmental, comparative, critical, defensive, or shaming thoughts? Do you replay things you or someone else did or said? What do your thoughts say when you make a mistake, or feel sad or lonely? What do your thoughts say when you accomplish something, or have impressed someone?

...How would it feel to hold a continuously loving, safe space for yourself? What might it feel like to acknowledge all this mental chatter, & choose not to follow where it leads? How much vitality could you potentially reclaim by recognizing the chatter's futility?

Observations

Begin again. Begin now. Just look & feel & listen.

Let's look a bit further…

Observe what you feed your system.

Do you drink alcohol often? Smoke? Consume illegal substances or habit-forming prescription drugs? Do you restrict/deny yourself nourishment? Binge & purge? Overeat? What types of foods & drinks do you consume? Are you honest with yourself & others about your behaviors in these areas? Do you have an oral fixation? Do you chew gum or eat hard candy often? Do you bite your nails or the insides of your lips or cheeks? Do you grind your teeth when you sleep?

…What might it feel like to nourish your body lovingly? Could you begin to teach yourself kindness by pausing when you discover yourself engaging in these behaviors, accepting your pain/fear/anxiety, forgiving yourself for harming the body, breathing consciously, & choosing something gentle & caring instead?

Observations

How restfully do you sleep? How do you feel when you wake? How is your energy level throughout the day?

…Can you find/create a safe place to sleep if you do not have one currently? Can you incorporate a calming ritual before bed which invites relaxation & trust?

What do you read? Watch? Listen to? Observe the types of language, tone, & energy you choose to feed your system. Observe the feelings they conjure. Try replacing something you read, watch, or listen to regularly for a few days with silent meditation, & observe any feelings that arise—the feelings you had likely been distracting yourself from with whatever habit(s) you removed.

…What might it feel like to nourish all of your senses positively? What might it reveal when you choose to prioritize silence over what you habitually consume?

Observations

Observe yourself honestly & without judgment. *Nothing is wrong with you & nothing is wrong.* Just look, feel, & quietly listen. Can you detect the anxiety & insecurity beneath your habits? Can you look further, beneath the anxiety? Can you accept your behaviors with patience & forgiveness & loving language? Can you begin to have a gentler, more nourishing relationship with your body?

Observations

Investigate your body. (Just look. Nothing is wrong.)

Do you persistently experience physical discomfort you can't seem to eradicate? Do you exhibit hypochondriac tendencies? Do you ever feel ill with worry or anxiety? Do physical symptoms distract you from being able to function?

…Can you give these physical symptoms attention through meditation—where you are not thinking about them & figuring them out, but where you are simply breathing into whatever physical & emotional sensory cues they are offering?

Observations

Observe your sexual activity. Are you uncomfortable with sex &/or intimacy? How does your current partner treat you? How do you treat him/her? Do you endure sex? Do you avoid sex entirely? Do you use sex for power? Pleasure? Attention? Subjugation? Distraction? Do you stifle or allow your expression? Do you orgasm? How do you talk to yourself in your head about your indulgent or prudent behaviors? Any judgments? Do you agree with your opinions?

…What might it feel like to fully love & appreciate your body, & fully enjoy connecting through sexuality? Can you forgive yourself for all past self-abandonment? Can you honor your body's requests, thereby teaching yourself trust? Can you be honest with your present partner about any discomfort you feel as soon as you feel it? Can you allow yourself to be seen & appreciated by another? Can you allow yourself pleasure? Can you find ways to sensually appreciate your body & show yourself love?

Observations

How critical are you of your physical self—this body you are wearing & its characteristics? Do you place more attention on how your body looks, or how it feels? Do you criticize your physical appearance & try to control or 'fix' it?

…What might complete self-acceptance feel like? Can you witness your self-judgment without believing it & becoming possessed by it? Can you commit to focusing on & honoring how you feel? Can you accept all the things you have conditioned yourself to judge, fix, despise, deny, or resist? Can you accept that right now you are truly absolutely perfect?

Observations

Observe secrets.

Do you still adhere to your family of origin's dysfunctional system? Are you still keeping secrets? Please observe any remaining dishonesty in your communication with yourself & others. What behaviors do you currently use to self-regulate when these secrets visit your thoughts? Can you acknowledge your behaviors with compassion? Can you apologize to the recipient(s) of your violence (including yourself) when you discover yourself behaving in violence, & employ love instead?

…What might it feel like to forgive yourself & others for *everything*? Can you meet your judgments with love? Can you begin to trust yourself, the earth that supports you, the universe that contains you? Can you begin to create a loving space in which you live—a home of truth & love within you & around you? Can you teach yourself, through love, that you are safe now?

Observations

Be loving to yourself & you will naturally behave intuitively toward whomever & whatever you encounter. Accept. Listen to your heart. Live from your heart. *You are made of love.*

* * * * * * * * * * * * * ** * * * * * * * *

Made in the USA
Las Vegas, NV
08 March 2022

45265976R00069